To our baby boy, Aiden, who in his own little way brings us joy and laughter.
- A. C.

Published by Mytogo Publishing 2022

Little Aiden - A Feelings Book for Toddlers

ISBN-13: 978-1-7387880-0-2

LITTLE AIDEN

A Feelings Book for Toddlers

Written by
Albert and Anna Choi

Illustrated by
Bettina Braskó

It is **OKAY** to have feelings.
Aiden feels them too.

Sometimes Aiden feels

RELAXED,

and that is **okay**.

Sometimes Aiden feels

EMBARRASSED,

and that is **okay**.

BRRRRT!

Sometimes Aiden feels

PROUD,

and that is **okay**.

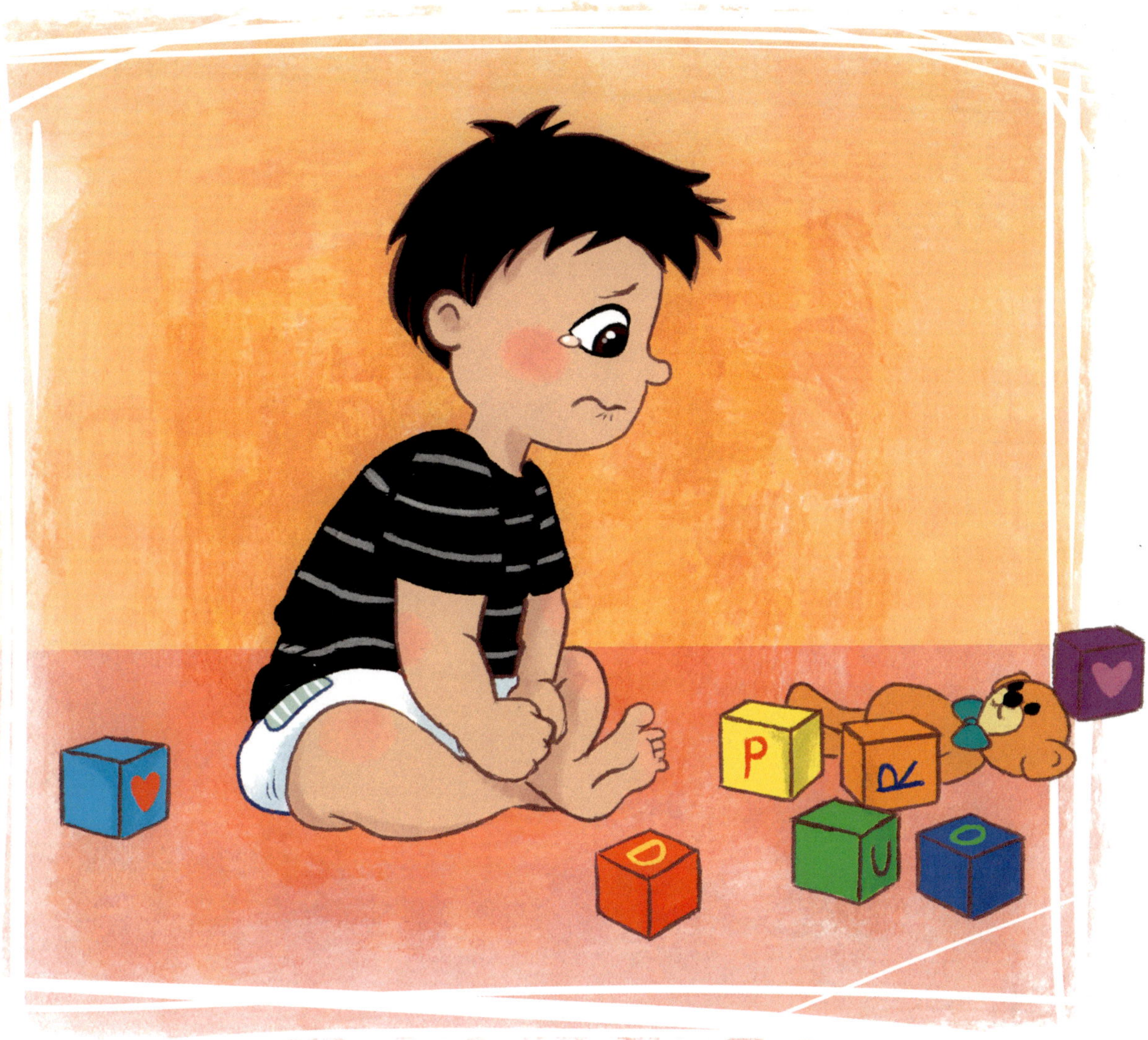

Sometimes Aiden feels

SAD,

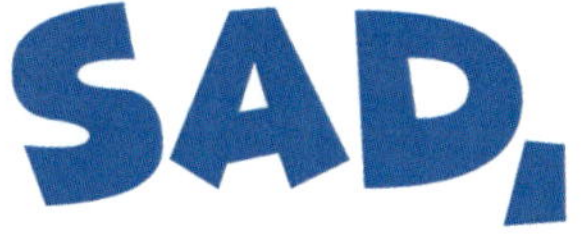

and that is **okay**.

Sometimes Aiden feels

FRUSTRATED . . .

and that is **okay**.

UH-OH!

Sometimes Aiden feels

HELPLESS,

and that is okay.

5:20

BAH!!
BUH!
BA-BAH!!
5:22

Sometimes Aiden feels . . .

5:22
ANGRY,
and that is okay.

Sometimes Aiden feels . . .

SILLY,
and that is okay.
MWAH!

Sometimes Aiden feels

CURIOUS . . .

and that is **okay**.

Sometimes Aiden feels

PLAYF

UL, and that is **okay**.

VROO

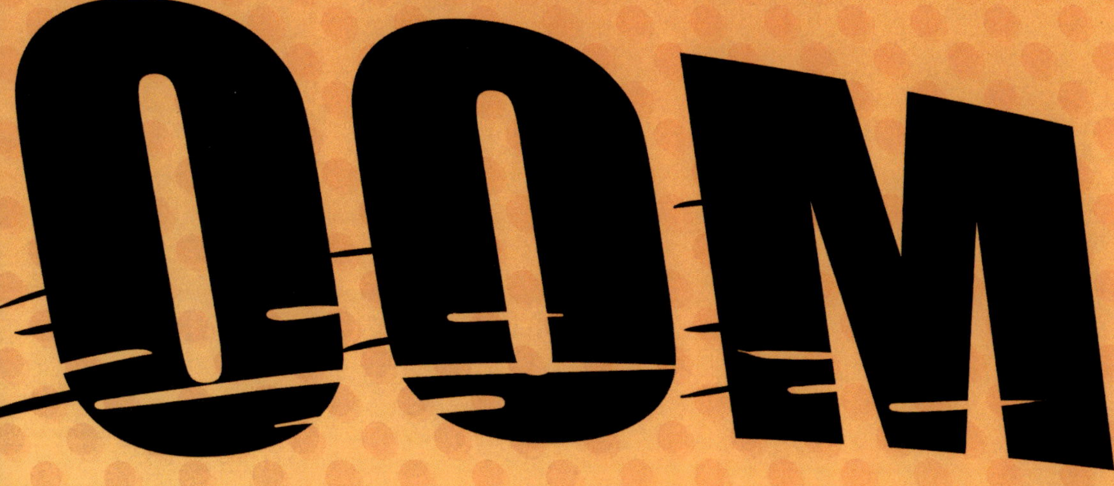

Sometimes Aiden feels

SCARED,

Wahh!!

and that is **okay**.

Sometimes Aiden feels **very**

HAPPY,

and that is okay.

Sometimes Aiden feels **very**

ED,
and that is okay.
zZZ

Aiden has **all** these feelings,

and they are **all okay**.

Do you have these feelings too?

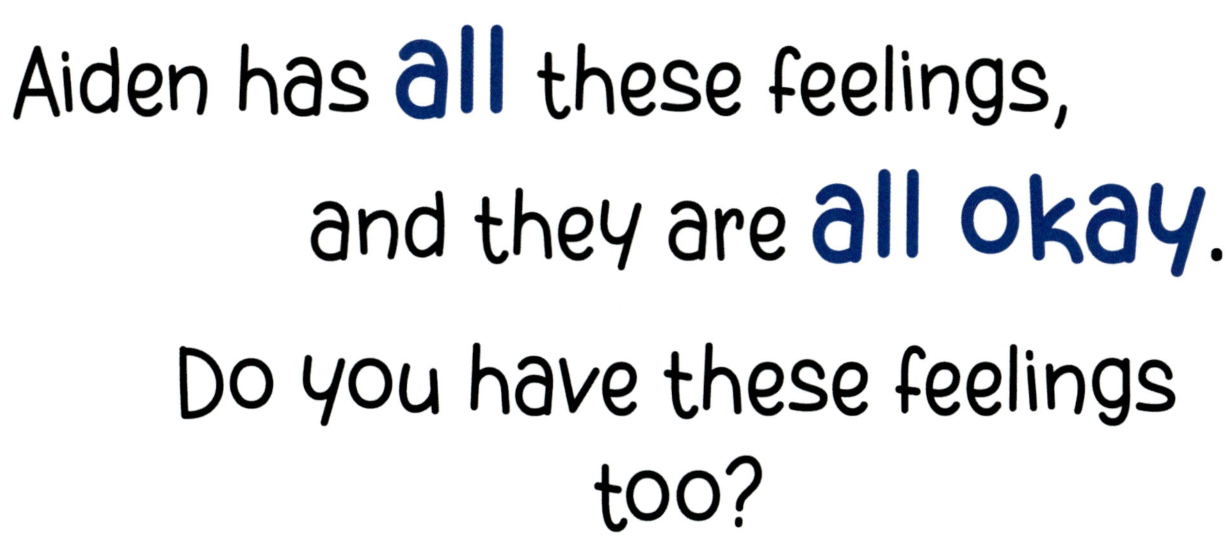

2
1
3

Dear Reader,

Thank you so much for reading this book. We hope you enjoyed the book and got some value out of it! If you did, please consider leaving a quick review on Amazon. Your feedback is very much appreciated. Thank you so much for your time.

ABOUT THE AUTHORS

Albert and Anna Choi are the parents of Aiden, the adorable little boy in this book. They love spending time together at nearby parks and playgrounds. Inspired by Aiden's daily adventures, both Albert and Anna set out to write a series of children's books based on values they wish to teach Aiden.

Buh! Buh!